WORLD WAR II

WEAPONS OF WORLD WAR II

by Clara MacCarald

FOCUS READERS®
VOYAGER

www.focusreaders.com

Copyright © 2023 by Focus Readers®, Lake Elmo, MN 55042. All rights reserved. No part of this book may be reproduced or utilized in any form or by any means without written permission from the publisher.

Focus Readers is distributed by North Star Editions:
sales@northstareditions.com | 888-417-0195

Produced for Focus Readers by Red Line Editorial.

Content Consultant: Dr. Gideon Mailer, Associate Professor of History, University of Minnesota Duluth

Photographs ©: Shutterstock Images, cover, 1, 4–5, 7, 8–9, 11, 13, 14–15, 20–21, 23, 25, 28–29, 31, 36–37, 38, 41, 42–43, 45; AP Images, 17, 27; ITAR/TASS News Agency/Alamy, 19; U.S. Maritime Commission/Library of Congress, 33; Fotosearch/Archive Photos/Getty Images, 35

Library of Congress Cataloging-in-Publication Data
Names: MacCarald, Clara, 1979- author.
Title: Weapons of World War II / Clara MacCarald.
Description: Lake Elmo, MN : Focus Readers, [2023] | Series: World War II | Includes index. | Audience: Grades 4-6
Identifiers: LCCN 2022010491 (print) | LCCN 2022010492 (ebook) | ISBN 9781637392843 (hardcover) | ISBN 9781637393369 (paperback) | ISBN 9781637394342 (pdf) | ISBN 9781637393888 (ebook)
Subjects: LCSH: Military weapons--History--20th century--Juvenile literature. | World War, 1939-1945--Equipment and supplies--Juvenile literature.
Classification: LCC UF500 .M33 2023 (print) | LCC UF500 (ebook) | DDC 355.8/2--dc23/eng/20220307
LC record available at https://lccn.loc.gov/2022010491
LC ebook record available at https://lccn.loc.gov/2022010492

Printed in the United States of America
Mankato, MN
082022

ABOUT THE AUTHOR
Clara MacCarald is a freelance writer with a master's degree in ecology and natural resources. She lives with her family in an off-grid house nestled in the forests of central New York. When not parenting her daughter, she spends her time writing nonfiction books for kids.

TABLE OF CONTENTS

CHAPTER 1
The Technology of War 5

CHAPTER 2
Guns and Grenades 9

CHAPTER 3
Tank Warfare 15

CHAPTER 4
War in the Air 21

A CLOSER LOOK
The Blitz 26

CHAPTER 5
War at Sea 29

A CLOSER LOOK
Kamikazes 34

CHAPTER 6
Atomic Bombs 37

CHAPTER 7
Postwar Impacts 43

Focus on Weapons of World War II • 46
Glossary • 47
To Learn More • 48
Index • 48

CHAPTER 1

THE TECHNOLOGY OF WAR

Weapons **technology** tends to advance during war. Each side tries to find more effective ways to fight. For example, during World War I (1914–1918), many battles took place in trenches dug into the ground. Soldiers fought with guns and **artillery**. The conflict also featured new types of vehicles. Early tanks barreled over the land between trenches. Airplanes shot guns and

During wars, countries often race to produce the most weapons.

dropped bombs. Submarines snuck up on ships to strike.

Weapon development continued after World War I ended. Germany and Japan, in particular, worked to create new technology. Both countries had plans to take over more territory. Their attempts at expansion led to another war.

World War II (1939–1945) began when Germany invaded Poland. Britain and France declared war on Germany soon after. The Soviet Union and the United States eventually joined Britain and France. Together, they were known as the Allies. Meanwhile, Italy and Japan sided with Germany. Those three countries formed the Axis powers. Many other countries fought in the war as well. Some joined the Allies. Others sided with the Axis powers. Massive battles raged around the world.

▲ By 1940, Germany had the biggest and strongest air force in Europe.

During World War II, trenches became much less important, especially in Europe. In addition to fighting on land, opponents clashed in the air or attacked one another at sea. Planes also battered enemy cities with bombs.

Eventually, better weapons production and technology helped the Allies win. But this victory came at a high cost. World War II became the bloodiest conflict in history. Deaths likely totaled more than 60 million. This number included both **civilians** and people in the military.

CHAPTER 2

GUNS AND GRENADES

Soldiers in World War II carried several kinds of weapons. They could have knives, pistols, or rifles. At the start of the war, most soldiers had to stop and reload their guns after each shot. Only the US Army regularly provided semiautomatic rifles to its troops. This type of rifle could reload itself after each shot. The soldier just had to pull the trigger. The M1 rifle could shoot eight times in a row before soldiers had to put in

Soldiers often carried many pounds of ammunition for their guns.

9

more **ammunition**. Later in the war, the German and Soviet armies also used large numbers of semiautomatic rifles.

Machine guns were even more powerful. These types of guns were automatic weapons. As long as its trigger remained pulled, a machine gun kept firing over and over until it ran out of ammunition. Machine guns could fire many shots very quickly. For example, the German MG42 could shoot 25 times per second.

Some machine guns were large and heavy. They needed several soldiers to operate them. Lighter machine guns could be used by one soldier, who propped the gun up on supports while firing it.

Machine guns could get quite hot while they fired. The MG42 gun overheated very quickly. A machine gun team would have to switch the hot

🔺 A machine gun fires bullets that are linked together in a belt.

barrel with a cool one to keep firing. British forces had the Bren. This machine gun fired less than half as fast as the MG42. However, it stayed cooler for longer.

A submachine gun was a kind of light machine gun. One soldier could hold it and use it like a rifle. Submachine guns didn't have a long range. But they worked well for fighting in close quarters.

Germany developed the first submachine gun during World War I. By the time World War II began, the US military had submachine guns as well. A popular type was known as the Tommy gun. It shot approximately 800 times per minute. The United States manufactured large numbers of these guns. The British and other Allied forces also used them. In 1943, the US military began using M3s, too. This type of submachine gun was cheaper and easier to make.

Soldiers also carried grenades. These small bombs were often thrown by hand. Many grenades sent out gas or shards of metal when they exploded. They could take out several enemy soldiers at once.

A mortar was a tube with metal legs that launched a bomb into the air. Mortars were easy for soldiers to carry and use. Other types of

When soldiers drop a shell into a mortar, a pin at the tube's bottom makes the shell explode.

artillery were bigger and heavier. Soldiers often used horses, trucks, or tractors to move them. These huge guns could fire large shells. They could shoot very long distances. The heaviest could hit a target more than 10 miles (16 km) away. Some large guns were specifically designed to take out tanks or planes.

CHAPTER 3

TANK WARFARE

Tanks played a major role in World War II. A small number of tanks had been used during World War I. However, these tanks moved slowly. And they often broke down. In the years leading up to World War II, Germany created new tanks called panzers. These tanks had stronger guns and stronger armor. They were also faster and more reliable.

Tanks are military vehicles with large guns and strong armor.

Germany used its improved tanks for a new kind of warfare. In the past, armies had mainly used tanks to support **infantry**. But Germany used its tanks to lead attacks. It formed groups of tanks that fought together. For example, Germany sent 2,000 tanks to invade Poland in September 1939. These tanks were backed up by 1,300 planes. This huge force quickly overwhelmed the Polish army.

This style of attack became known as a blitzkrieg. That word means "lightning war" in German. Huge groups of tanks and planes swept in and crushed enemy armies. Germany won many battles this way.

In 1940, for example, Germany attacked France. French tanks outnumbered the German tanks. But the French tanks were slow. They also fought in much smaller groups. As a result, the German tanks defeated them.

▲ Panzers played a key role in Germany's invasion of Poland in 1939.

Panzers also pushed through other Allied defenses. Germany used panzers to invade the Soviet Union in June 1941. At first, victory came easily. In July, the Germans surrounded Soviet troops and forced them to surrender. However, new Soviet tanks surprised the Germans. These KV-1 tanks had heavy armor. They could block shells and stop panzers.

Weather posed problems for the panzers as well. Roads filled with mud and snow, stalling the tanks. The delay gave the Soviets time to bring in more soldiers. They began pushing back the German invaders.

Allied tank forces improved throughout the war. Both the US Sherman tank and the Soviet T-34 could match lighter types of panzers. In response, Germans designed two new tank types to fight the T-34. The Panther was heavy but fast. It had thick armor and powerful guns. The Tiger was even bigger and stronger. But it could not travel as fast or as far.

In the summer of 1943, German and Soviet tanks clashed in the Battle of Kursk. German Panthers and Tigers fought against new and improved T-34s. Germany lost. After the battle, Soviet forces started pushing the Germans back. The Soviets were able to produce far more tanks than their opponents. These large numbers of

▲ The Battle of Kursk was the largest tank battle in history. It involved approximately 6,000 tanks.

tanks also helped the Soviets win victories in Poland and Japan.

Armies on both sides developed weapons to use against tanks. Infantry used rocket launchers to shoot shells or grenades that could pierce a tank's armor. Armies also built tank destroyers. These vehicles carried antitank guns. As tank armor improved, antitank guns grew bigger. They also fired new types of ammunition.

CHAPTER 4

WAR IN THE AIR

Airplane designs had advanced by World War II as well. Militaries developed new fighters and bombers. These planes could fly farther without refueling. They also carried better weapons. Bombs grew bigger and more destructive. So did bombers. They could drop tons of explosives.

The best fighters were streamlined planes with powerful engines. Early in the war, Britain's Spitfire could reach speeds of 360 miles per hour

The Hurricane (top) and Spitfire (bottom) fighters helped Britain defeat the German air force.

(580 km/h). Japan's Zero had less power. But it could turn quickly and travel long distances. Near the war's end, Germany put small numbers of the first jet fighters into combat. The jets could fly up to 540 miles per hour (870 km/h).

Fighters could carry machine guns, rockets, or cannons. But hitting a rapidly moving object with ammunition was difficult. So, militaries created shells that could sense when they came near a plane. These shells could explode and cause damage even without a direct hit.

To defend against planes, an army had to know where they were. Before the war, scientists had invented radar. This system used radio waves to find objects. Militaries used it to watch for airplanes. Britain built a radar system along its coast. Each station could detect planes up to 80 miles (129 km) away.

Radar played a key part in the Battle of Britain in 1940. German planes hoped to crush the British air force. However, radar allowed British airplanes to find and challenge the attackers. Britain also had the advantage of better planes. One was the Spitfire fighter. Its shape and engine allowed it to fly very fast and very high. As a result, Spitfires shot down many German fighters.

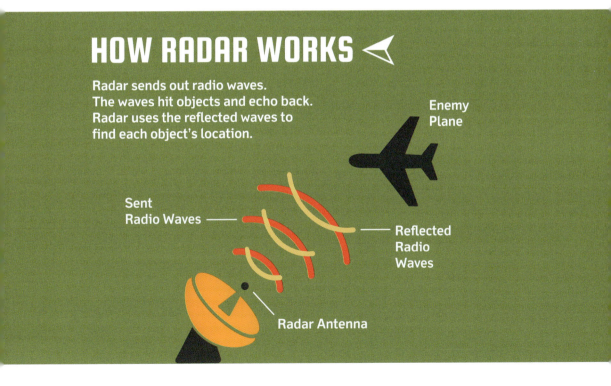

HOW RADAR WORKS

Radar sends out radio waves. The waves hit objects and echo back. Radar uses the reflected waves to find each object's location.

Enemy Plane

Sent Radio Waves

Reflected Radio Waves

Radar Antenna

Britain's Hurricane fighters were slower. But they carried several machine guns. They could split German bombers in half.

Britain's strong defense kept Germany from invading as planned. Instead, German planes bombed cities throughout Britain. They hoped to scare British leaders into surrendering.

During World War II, bombers could aim at specific targets, such as factories or military bases. However, many planes carried out area bombing. They rained bombs on cities. It was easier to hit a city with factories in it than it was to hit the factories themselves. Both the Axis and

CONSIDER THIS

How would flying high give airplanes an advantage during battles?

▲ A tail gunner shoots at enemies from the back of a fighter while a pilot flies the plane.

Allies used this **strategy**. Area bombing killed and wounded huge numbers of civilians.

In 1944, Germany began using a long-range rocket, the V-2. The V-2 could fly 120 miles (190 km) at great speeds. It had an automatic system for directing itself to the target. The Germans fired V-2 rockets at distant cities. The attacks seemed to come out of nowhere.

A CLOSER LOOK

THE BLITZ

In September 1940, Germany began dropping bombs on London and other British cities. These attacks were known as the Blitz. German planes attacked some military targets. But they also bombed many civilian neighborhoods.

Britain was prepared for an air attack. Its government sent some people, mainly children, to the countryside, where attacks were less likely. It also gave out gas masks to people in cities. Wearing these masks protected people from bombs that released poison.

For 57 nights in a row, London came under attack. The government ordered people to cover or turn off all lights. The darkness made it harder for German bombers to find targets. As enemy planes approached, sirens warned people to seek shelter. Many civilians retreated underground into London's subway stations. Others hid in bomb

▲ Plymouth was one of the British cities hit hardest by German air raids.

shelters. These metal structures could hold two to six people. They helped people stay safe if a building collapsed.

During the Blitz, German planes dropped more than 220,500 pounds (100,000 kg) of explosives on 16 British cities. Thousands of people were killed and wounded. In London alone, 30,000 people died. German leaders hoped all this death and destruction would make Britain give up. But the British kept on fighting. In May 1941, Germany ended the Blitz. It prepared to invade the Soviet Union instead.

CHAPTER 5

WAR AT SEA

Airplanes became an important part of sea warfare during World War II. Planes took off and landed from the decks of large ships called aircraft carriers. Aircraft carriers allowed a fleet to bring along its own air force. Planes no longer needed to go back to land to refuel. The United States and Japan both used aircraft carriers to fight battles in the Pacific Ocean.

Aircraft carriers allowed armies to fight battles in the ocean many miles from land.

Fighting at sea often featured submarines, too. However, these submarines spent most of the time above the water. On the surface, the submarines used diesel engines. They could move fast. And they could cover long distances without having to refuel. Underwater, the submarines used electric batteries. They moved very slowly, and their power ran out quickly. To recharge their batteries, submarines had to return to the surface.

Even so, submarines were still a threat. They attacked and sank many ships. Submarines often targeted supply ships. This strategy weakened enemy armies. Without fuel or materials for factories, enemies would run out of weapons.

The devastating attacks of German U-boats were one example. These submarines sank hundreds of British and US merchant ships early in the war. In the Pacific, US submarines

▲ U-boats float in a harbor in Germany.

destroyed many Japanese warships and shipping boats.

Ships used radar to watch for enemy attacks. But radar doesn't reach far below the water's surface. So, ships turned to sonar. This system is similar to radar. But it uses sound waves instead of radio waves. Sonar technology helped ships find submarines.

Ships, planes, and submarines could carry **torpedoes**. Japan had the deadliest torpedoes. They were fast and powerful. They could strike targets from more than 10 miles (16 km) away. And they could split a ship in half. These weapons helped Japan win many battles against the Allies.

Landing craft also played an important role during World War II. These vehicles helped armies carry out sea-based attacks. They transported troops and equipment from ships to enemy shores. A large landing craft could hold up to 18 Sherman tanks and 160 soldiers. Landing craft could also carry guns or rockets. They shot at enemies to provide cover as their own troops went ashore.

The Allies used landing craft for several battles. The most famous took place on June 6, 1944. On that day, the Allies invaded Normandy,

▲ On D-Day, thousands of ships and landing craft brought soldiers to beaches in Normandy, France.

France. The attack was known as D-Day. It was the largest **assault** by sea in history. More than 150,000 Allied troops landed on Normandy's beaches. From the shore, the troops fought their way inland, taking back land in **occupied** France. Their success was a turning point in the war against Germany.

US troops also used landing craft in the Pacific. They moved from island to island as they fought their way toward Japan.

A CLOSER LOOK

KAMIKAZES

Kamikaze attacks turned airplanes into weapons. Pilots purposely crashed their planes into enemy ships or other targets. The crashes did massive amounts of damage. They also killed the pilots.

The word *kamikaze* means "sacred winds." The term comes from Japanese myth. In the 1200s, the Mongols gathered huge fleets to invade Japan. A legend says that the Japanese emperor summoned a storm that destroyed the ships and saved Japan. Near the end of World War II, Japan's emperor used this myth to call Japanese pilots to crash their planes. He asked them to defend their country.

The first kamikaze attack on Allied ships happened in October 1944. Kamikaze planes carried lots of bombs and gas tanks to increase the damage they caused. And they moved very

▲ A kamikaze plane plunges toward an aircraft carrier.

fast. Allied forces struggled to shoot them down before they crashed.

By the end of the war, kamikaze attacks had sunk more than 30 ships. They had killed more than 7,000 Allied soldiers. More than 3,000 kamikaze pilots also died. Most of the pilots were 17 to 24 years old. Some were eager to sacrifice themselves. Others didn't want to die but felt they couldn't refuse the emperor's order.

After the war, some Japanese people saw kamikazes as heroes. Others disagreed. They felt it was wrong to have pilots kill themselves.

CHAPTER 6

ATOMIC BOMBS

World War II featured the first use of atomic bombs. In 1938, scientists had discovered **nuclear fission**. They calculated that splitting an atom would create a massive amount of energy. In 1939, German scientists began working on using this process to create weapons. Scientists who had escaped Germany warned US President Franklin Delano Roosevelt about this work.

At the Hanford Site, US scientists worked to produce fuel for atomic bombs.

Roosevelt gave his approval to start atomic research in the United States.

Scientists worked to create both a bomb and its fuel. They needed the fuel to start a **chain reaction** inside the bomb. This reaction would cause a huge explosion.

Both Germany and Japan had their own atomic programs. But neither received much government

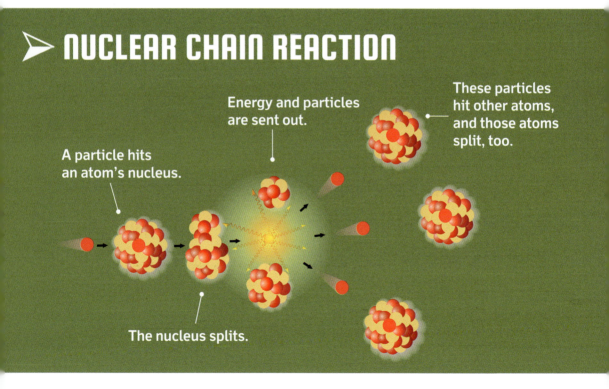

NUCLEAR CHAIN REACTION

A particle hits an atom's nucleus.

Energy and particles are sent out.

These particles hit other atoms, and those atoms split, too.

The nucleus splits.

funding or support. The United States, however, put together a huge effort. It hired more than 100,000 people to work for a program called the Manhattan Project.

Roosevelt died in April 1945. Harry S. Truman became the new president. By this time, scientists at the Manhattan Project had developed two bomb designs. The first kind of bomb shot one bit of nuclear fuel into another. Together, these two fuels started a chain reaction. Using this method, scientists built a bomb called Little Boy. The second design was trickier. It surrounded nuclear fuel with regular explosives. A bomb called Fat Man used this method. Scientists tested this type of bomb on July 16 in a desert in New Mexico. The massive explosion was even larger than expected.

Germany had surrendered back in May. Japan was losing in the Pacific. However, it continued to fight. US planes had been bombing Japanese cities. These attacks killed hundreds of thousands of people. Still, Japan fought on. US forces prepared to invade the country. Experts predicted that millions of people would die or be wounded.

The Soviet Union had agreed to start helping the United States fight Japan in mid-August. However, Truman wasn't sure he wanted this help. US and Soviet leaders didn't trust one another. Truman decided to rely on his country's new atomic bombs instead. He hoped they would bring the war to a faster end.

On August 6, a US bomber dropped Little Boy on the city of Hiroshima, Japan. The huge explosion killed at least 70,000 people. Many survivors suffered terrible burns or **radiation sickness**. More than 200,000 of these people would die later on.

▲ In Nagasaki, the atomic bomb damaged an area covering 43 square miles (111 sq km).

On August 9, the United States dropped Fat Man on Nagasaki, Japan. At least 40,000 people died instantly. Over the next few years, wounds or sickness caused by the bomb killed thousands more.

Japan agreed to surrender on August 14. On September 2, World War II officially ended. Today, people still disagree about whether dropping the atomic bombs was necessary.

CHAPTER 7

POSTWAR IMPACTS

Nuclear weapons played a part in ending World War II. However, they led to other problems after it. The United States and the Soviet Union had been wartime allies. But after World War II, tensions rose between them. This era became known as the Cold War.

During the Cold War, the United States and the Soviet Union did not fight each other directly. By 1949, the Soviet Union had developed its own

The United States and the Soviet Union continued testing new types of nuclear weapons.

nuclear weapons. The devastation in Japan had shown that a nuclear war could destroy the world. So, countries used their weapons as threats. They tried to build the most weapons. And they found ways to shoot long distances. Over the years, several other countries have acquired their own nuclear weapons.

Weapons technology from World War II has also inspired less-violent inventions. The V-2 led to rockets used for spaceflight. Also, people began using radar to forecast the weather.

The weapons of World War II changed the world in many ways. And they continue to impact

> **CONSIDER THIS**

Which weapon used during World War II do you think has had the biggest impact on life today? Why?

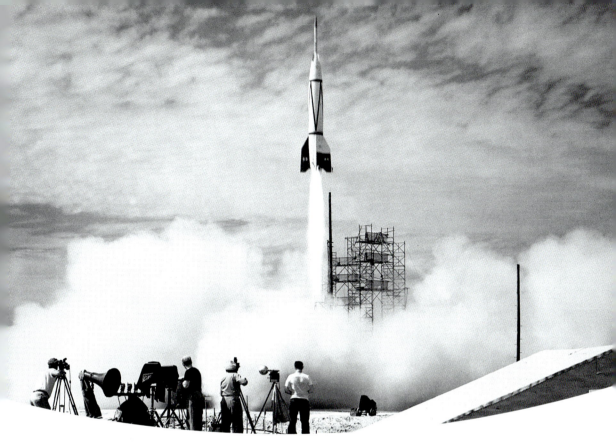

▲ Studying V-2 missiles helped US scientists build rockets that launched spaceships.

the world today. For example, some of the bombs dropped during World War II did not explode. Unexploded bombs can be very dangerous. Trained experts must deal carefully with them. Otherwise, they can blow up and hurt people. Leftover bombs have killed hundreds of people since the war. And more are still being found.

FOCUS ON
WEAPONS OF WORLD WAR II

Write your answers on a separate piece of paper.

1. Write a letter to a friend describing what you learned about tanks in World War II.

2. Do you think it's right for an army to carry out attacks that can hurt civilians? Why or why not?

3. What was a blitzkrieg attack?
   - **A.** a fast attack made with many tanks and airplanes
   - **B.** an attack in which bombers purposely target civilians
   - **C.** an attack in which pilots purposely crash their airplanes

4. What type of weapon is a submachine gun?
   - **A.** an automatic weapon
   - **B.** a semiautomatic weapon
   - **C.** a tank destroyer

Answer key on page 48.

GLOSSARY

ammunition
Bullets or shells that are shot from a gun.

artillery
Large guns, often mounted on wheels.

assault
An attack on an area that is under enemy control.

chain reaction
A series of events in which each action causes new actions.

civilians
People who are not in the military.

infantry
Soldiers who fight on foot.

nuclear fission
The splitting of an atom's nucleus.

occupied
Under the control of a foreign country or invading army.

radiation sickness
A dangerous illness caused by being exposed to nuclear energy or particles.

strategy
An action or plan designed to achieve a specific goal.

technology
Machines and devices created using science.

torpedoes
Tube-shaped bombs that move and explode underwater.

TO LEARN MORE

BOOKS

Gale, Ryan. *The Manhattan Project*. Minneapolis: Abdo Publishing, 2021.

Langley, Andrew. *Hiroshima and Nagasaki*. North Mankato, MN: Capstone Publishing, 2018.

Murray, Laura K. *World War II Technology*. Minneapolis: Abdo Publishing, 2018.

NOTE TO EDUCATORS

Visit **www.focusreaders.com** to find lesson plans, activities, links, and other resources related to this title.

INDEX

aircraft carriers, 29
airplanes, 5, 7, 13, 16, 21–24, 26–27, 29, 32, 34, 40
antitank guns, 19
artillery, 5, 13
atomic bombs, 37–41

grenades, 12, 19

kamikazes, 34–35

landing craft, 32–33

machine guns, 10–11, 22, 24
mortars, 12

nuclear weapons, 44

radar, 22–23, 31, 44
rockets, 22, 25, 32, 44

semiautomatic rifles, 9–10
sonar, 31
submachine guns, 11–12
submarines, 6, 30–32

tanks, 5, 13, 15–19, 32
torpedoes, 32

U-boats, 30

Answer Key: 1. Answers will vary; 2. Answers will vary; 3. A; 4. A